CW01432393

Rhona Snelling

Inside
Number 8

DELTA Publishing

You can listen to *Inside Number 8* using the free DELTA Augmented app – you'll also find fun interactive activities!

Download the free DEL-TA Augmented app onto your device

Start picture recognition and scan the **contents page**

Download files and use them now or save them for later

1st edition   1 5 4 3 2 1 | 2026 25 24 23 22

Delta Publishing, 2022
www.deltapublishing.co.uk

© Ernst Klett Sprachen GmbH, Rotebühlstraße 77, 70178 Stuttgart, 2022

Author: Rhona Snelling
Editor: Kate Baade
Cover and layout: Andreas Drabarek
Illustrations: Gustavo Mazali
Design: Datagroup int, Timisoara
Cover picture: Gustavo Mazali
Printing and binding: Plump Druck & Medien GmbH, Rheinbreitbach

ISBN 978-3-12-501155-7

Contents

Abbreviations

sb   somebody
sth   something

Photos:

6 123RF.com (primulakat), Nidderau; **17** 123RF.com (onyxprj), Nidderau; **49** 123RF.com (vanreeell), Nidderau; **58** 123RF.com (iulika1), Nidderau; **59.1** 123RF.com (angyee054), Nidderau; **59.2** 123RF.com (djvstock), Nidderau

Before you start

1. The title of the story is 'Inside Number 8'. What do you think this refers to? Where do you think the story is set?

2. Look at the illustrations of the main characters in the story. Think of two questions to ask each character. Read the story and try to answer your questions.

3. Look at these two illustrations from the story. What do you think the story is about?

Chapter 1

Jay stops at the gate. He looks at the garden. The garden is small, but there are trees everywhere. There are big trees at the back. There are small trees at the front. There are trees on the walls. There are more trees in front of the walls. There are trees next to the path. There are trees on top of trees. They are everywhere! "It isn't a garden. It's a forest!" thinks Jay. Where is Esme? He looks at the garden again. He can't see Esme. Where *is* she?

"Nice to see you! Nice to see you!"

Captain P flies to Jay and sits on his shoulder. Jay smiles.

"Nice to see you! Nice to see you!" Captain P sings in Jay's ear and dances on Jay's shoulder.

"CAPTAIN P! NO! COME HERE! NOW!" shouts Esme.

Captain P flies to Esme and sits on her hand. Esme talks to Captain P. Jay can't hear the words. Captain P nods his head. Then he flies to a tree. He is a big, beautiful bird. He is red, yellow, green and blue. There are lots of other birds in the tree. They are small and brown. The birds make noises and jump in and out of the tree. Are they singing? Are they dancing? Captain P winks at Jay.

"I'm very sorry, Jay. Are you okay? Come in. Open the gate. Come in!" says Esme.

Jay enters the garden. He gives Esme a big birthday card and some flowers. The birthday card has the number '68' on it.

"For me? Oh, thank you! They're lovely!" says Esme. "I've got a present for you. Are you hungry?" Esme points to a table next to the gate. There are two small cakes on the table.

Jay smiles again. Esme makes amazing cakes.

"This one is for your dad. This one is for you, Jay. It's your favourite – chocolate. And *this* is a present for you. It's from my last holiday. What do you think?"

9 **to smile** to move the corners of your mouth up, because you are happy – 10 **to sing** to make music with your voice – 14 **to nod** to move your head up and down because you agree, understand or want to say "yes" – 18 **to wink** to quickly close and open one eye

Esme always gives Jay the same present from her holidays. It is always a snow globe. Jay looks at it. There are some mountains behind a lake. The water is a bright green colour. There's a boat on the lake. Jay shakes the globe and … there is snow everywhere. Jay smiles and watches the scene. "I would love to see snow," thinks Jay.

"Well, yes. There isn't any snow *here*, Jay. There *is* snow – real snow – in other countries. Would you like a trip to a country with snow?" Esme asks.

Jay smiles. Esme is always kind. She always understands. Jay shakes the globe again. Then he walks through the gate and down the steps.

---

20 **snow globe** a small, glass object which contains a scene, some liquid, and very small white pieces (like snow) – 23 **scene** the action in the snow globe

Think about it...

What presents do you usually give to friends on their birthday?

Chapter 2

The steps are on the outside of the building. Jay walks from the garden on the roof down to the second floor. Jay lives on this floor with his dad. It's a big, comfortable apartment. Esme lives on her own now. She lives on the first floor and the ground floor. There is another garden on the ground floor. This has got lots of trees, too. Jay opens the door to the apartment and walks into the kitchen.

"Finally! You're late for lunch – again!" says Jay's dad. He looks at the two cakes and then he looks at Jay. Jay has got chocolate on his face. And his glasses. And his hands. And his T-shirt. And in his hair. "Oh, is *that* your lunch?" laughs his dad.

Jay nods and give his dad the other cake. Jay's dad smells the cake. "Mmmmm, lemons!" He takes a big bite and gives Jay the thumbs up sign. Jay returns the thumbs up sign.

"Oh, you've got another snow globe. Esme is very kind! How many have you got now? Is it ten?" says Jay's dad.

---

25 **finally** after a long time – 30 **to bite** to use your teeth to eat sth

Jay shakes his head and shows seven fingers. Then he shakes his head quickly and shows eight fingers.

"Eight! So, this is number eight. It's very nice. Look at the mountains and look at the snow! Beautiful! It's different to our country, eh?" says Jay's dad. "Wash your hands and then it's lunch … or maybe more cake."

Jake takes the snow globe to his bedroom. It's a sunny room with a big window. There are seven other snow globes on the top shelf above his desk. He picks up each snow globe and reads the number on the bottom. *1, 2, 3, 4, 5, 6, 7*. Yes, there are now eight snow globes. Jay writes '8' on the bottom of the new snow globe. He puts it carefully on the shelf and smiles at his collection. Then he picks up number 1 and shakes it. He quickly picks up and shakes each snow globe. He laughs at the snow.

Jay's dad walks into Jay's bedroom.

"Brrr. It's cold! Ah! It's cold, because it's *snowing*! Come on, Jay. Hands! Lunch! Cake! I'm hungry!" he says.

Jay nods and follows his dad into the kitchen.

Think about it …

Do you collect anything?

What are your favourite things in your bedroom?

1 **to shake your head** to move your head from side to side because you want to say "no" – 5 **eh** used to ask sb to agree with you – 9 **to pick sth up** to take sth in your hand(s) – 12 **carefully** in a careful way – 12 **collection** a group of similar things – 13 **to shake** to quickly move sth up and down or side to side

Chapter 3

The kitchen is a small room. There is a cooker, a sink and some cupboards. There is a table with two chairs next to the fridge. Jay and his dad have breakfast here every morning. Today's breakfast is early, because today is an important day. Jay's dad has got a new job in the city centre.

Jay's dad puts on his coat and opens the kitchen door. It's time to go. Jay is putting some food in boxes and then in the fridge. He looks at his dad.

"Good boy! Thank you, Jay. Now, are you OK in the apartment? Do you want to come with me? Go to the museum or a library? Or maybe – oh, Esme!" says Jay's dad.

Esme is standing at the open door.

"Good morning! Look at your dad, Jay! He looks very smart!!" says Esme.

"Good morning, Esme! Thank you. Please come in. Do you want some breakfast?" asks Jay's dad.

"No, thanks. I'm busy today. I'm *very* busy. Look at my 'to do' list!" says Esme. She shows Jay's dad a long piece of paper. "I need an assistant today. Captain P is away today." Her face is sad.

Jay's dad smiles. He has got an idea.

"Don't worry! I have the perfect solution", he says. Then he coughs and speaks in a formal voice: "Esme, I'd like to introduce you to your new assistant. This is Jay. Jay is an excellent young man. He is polite and friendly. Jay, this is Esme. Esme is a *very* important person. She helps everyone. She is *very* wise and *very* kind."

Jay and Esme laugh and shake hands.

"Get your coat, Jay! Don't put the food in the fridge. You and Esme have a busy day today. The food is now your lunch. Here you are, Esme. Let's go!" says Jay's dad.

---

13 **smart** very nice, tidy and clean – 22 **to cough** to quickly move a lot of air out of your mouth (because you have a cold or you want to say sth important) – 22 **formal** important or official – 25 **wise** able to understand things or give advice because of years of experience and knowledge

The three of them leave the apartment and walk down the steps. The bus stop is opposite Esme's house, so they wait together. Jays' dad is worried about his new job, but Esme tells him lots of jokes. They laugh together. The bus arrives and Jay's dad is still laughing. He waves bye. Esme and Jay wave back.

Esme shows Jay her 'to do' list:

1 go to the park
2 practise the '180'
3 have fun

Jay smiles and runs to the house. He loves the park.

---

4 **joke** sth you say to make sb laugh – 5 **still** a situation that is continuing – 5 **wave** a hand movement to say "hello" or "bye"

Do you make 'to do' lists?
What's on your 'to do' list today?

Chapter 4

The park is busy today. Jay and Esme often ride their bikes to the park. Jay's bike is an old BMX. He loves it. It's red, yellow and blue. They watch some boys and girls ride their bikes. They go fast and they do jumps. They're very good. One boy can't do the 180 jump. He looks angry. Then he rides his bike to Esme and Jay. His friends follow him.

"What are you doing here? Can we help you?" asks the boy. The boys and girls laugh.

Eight boys and girls stand around Esme and Jay. Jay smiles at them. No one smiles at Jay. He looks at Esme.

"Hello! I'm Esme. This is my friend, Jay. *We* can help *you*. You are an excellent BMX rider, but the 180 is difficult. Move your shoulder before you jump. Then the bike turns, because it follows your shoulder," says Esme.

---

22 **jump** the action of going up into the air – 30 **BMX** 'bicycle motocross': a type of bike used for races and freestyle – 30 **rider** sb who rides a bike (or a horse)

Esme looks at Jay and says "You can do the 180, Jay. Show your new friends."

Then she checks Jay's helmet and whispers "You are the *best* BMX rider here! Do one 'bunny hop'. Then, do the '180'!"

Jay smiles. He's excited now. Esme thinks he is *the best*! He rides his bike fast and does a bunny hop. He pulls the front wheel up and then he pulls the back wheel up. Then, he pushes the bike down – the front and back wheels go down together. Perfect! The boys and girls are very quiet. This small boy on the old BMX is *good*. Two boys are making a video of Jay with their phones.

Now it's time for the 180. Jay is smiling. This is fun! First, he moves his shoulder left and pulls the front wheel up. Then he quickly pulls the back wheel up and pushes it right. Jay and his bike move 180 degrees through the air. Perfect! Then he does *another* 180. Perfect again!

The boys and girls aren't quiet now. They're shouting and calling Jay's name. They run to Jay. They ask him lots of questions. They want to know everything about him. The boys show Jay the video of his jumps. They take selfies with him.

Esme smiles. She prepares the food from Jay's dad. The new friends sit together. The boys and girls have got snacks, too. So, they share their food and have a big lunch.

After lunch, they teach Jay new jumps. They ride each other's bikes. They have races. They show Jay videos of BMX competitions. They find out a 'bunny hop' is called a 'J-hop' in America. They all laugh about the name. The new friends have a great day together.

Esme watches them. She looks at her 'to do' list. She draws a big tick next to the three points. It's time to go now.

The new friends are sad and happy. What a day! They say bye.

---

3 **helmet** safety hat for sport – 3 **to whisper** to speak in a low, quiet voice – 29 **tick** mark that shows sth is correct or complete

Later, Jay goes to bed with a big smile on his face. Jay's dad looks at his happy son and also smiles. "No bad dreams tonight!" he thinks. He turns off the light and closes the door.

Think about it...

What sports do you enjoy doing or watching? Why?

Chapter 5

The door opens and Captain P flies into Esme's kitchen.

"Nice to see you! Nice to see you!" he sings to Esme.

Captain P is very excited. He is *always* excited about trips. He flies left and right, up and down. He turns over and over in the air. He flies left and right again. He's fast. There is a flash of colour: red, yellow, and blue. Captain P is now wearing a pilot uniform. He's got a hat and a smart jacket. He speaks to his passenger.

"Ladies and gentlemen, this is your captain speaking. Welcome to today's flight. We are ready for take off. Put your safety belts on. Please put …"

"Captain P … ," begins Esme.

" … your bags under your seats. There are snacks and …," Captain P continues.

---

23 **flash** bright light that you see for a few seconds

"Captain P! There aren't any seats. There aren't any snacks. We've got an important job. Please can we go?" says Esme.

Captain P nods. Esme is right. They have got an important job. They need to go. Now. He flies around Esme in a small circle. He flies fast. Very fast. There are flashes of red, yellow, and blue. More and more flashes. Then there is silence. Esme isn't worried. She closes her eyes and smiles. They're on their way.

Esme opens her eyes. She can see the different countries in the world. They fly past her … or does she fly past them? There are more flashes of red, yellow and blue. Then there are more countries. Esme has got friends in every country in the world. She smiles and waves. Maybe her friends can see her? Maybe they're thinking of her at this moment? Then the flashes of colours stop. There's a noise. It's like a door opening.

"We're here!" Captain P says.

At the same time, there is a flash of light in Jay's bedroom. He wakes up. He's worried. He sits up in bed. Is it another bad dream? He looks at his clock. It's 01:23. He looks at his snow globes. They are flashing slowly. The first one flashes red. Then the second one flashes red. He counts the snow globes as they flash: *one, two, three, four, five, six, seven, eight*. Then they all flash yellow. Jay isn't worried anymore. He smiles. It's Esme and Captain P. This always happens when they go on a trip.

"Where are they? I would like to go with them one day," Jay thinks. He lies down and goes to sleep. Then one snow globe flashes blue. It's number seven and it shows a forest.

---

6 **silence** no noise – 8 **way** journey from one place to another

Think about it...

Where do you think Esme and Captain P are going? What do you think is their important job?

Chapter 6

"A forest is a fantastic place, but a rainforest is awesome!" says
Captain P. "Look at it!"

Captain P and Esme are standing in the middle of a rainforest.
They are very small next to the tall trees. Esme looks around her.
There are trees and plants everywhere. The trees touch over their
heads and make a ceiling of green. There is the soft sound of
rain. It's warm and the air is wet. There are sounds from different
animals in the rainforest. Then there is the sound of Captain P.

"Nice to see you! Nice to see you!" he sings in a loud voice.
A small group of birds fly down to meet Captain P. They are
old friends and they have a long conversation. There is lots of
laughing. Then the friends sing and fly in circles together.

Esme walks into the forest and Captain P flies after her. He
stops and talks to other friends on the way. Their job is to check

27 **voice** the sound sb makes when they speak

eight trees in different countries around the world. Today, they are checking number 7 in this rainforest. They see the tree, but they see someone is already with the tree.

Esme and Captain P see a boy standing in front of it. The tree and the boy are about the same size. The boy is chatting to the tree. The tree is chatting back. It changes into different colours: red, green, gold, purple, yellow, orange, pink, silver, and blue. It makes a low sound similar to a happy cat. It moves slowly from side to side.

"They're having a conversation!" whispers Esme to Captain P.

"What are you doing here? Can I help you?" asks the boy.

"The same questions…," says Esme. "Well, we're here to visit this tree. We need to check the tree is well and happy, because …"

"Yes, it is. Do you know there are special trees all over the world? This is one. Isn't it beautiful? The trees talk to each other. They look after each other. They're our friends, too. They take care of people, because they bring us clean air and water. We need trees," says the boy.

They hear a woman's voice a long way away. She's calling the boy.

"OK, that's my mum. I need to go now. Bye!" The boy waves to the tree and walks away. The tree changes to a bright gold colour for a few seconds and then changes green.

Captain P and Esme look at each other.

"What a perfect description!" says Esme.

Number seven is fine. They can go home now.

"Please prepare for departure," begins Captain P. "We're leaving in one, two, three, four, five."

---

5 **to chat** to talk in a friendly style – 27 **departure** the moment when sb leaves one place to go to another specific place

Think about it...

What do you know about rainforests?
Is there a forest near where you live?

Chapter 7

"Five things, Jay. Can you see *five* things in your bedroom?" asks Jay's dad.

Jay looks at his dad. He feels hot. He's worried. He remembers …

"Jay? Look at me," says his dad. "It's a bad dream, Jay. You're in your bedroom. We're safe. Everything is OK. Now, look at your bedroom. Can you see five things in your bedroom? I can. 1 Your bed – easy! 2 There's your clock. 3 There are your snow globes."

Jay looks at the bed and the clock. It's 01:10. He looks at his snow globes. He gets up and walks to the shelves. He picks up the first snow globe and shakes it. He puts it carefully back on the shelf and then picks up the next one. He repeats this with all the snow globes. He feels better.

"4 There's the big window. 5 There's my dad!" thinks Jay. He smiles at his dad. Everything *is* OK.

Jay lies down again and closes his eyes. His dad waits until Jay is sleeping. Then he quietly leaves Jay's bedroom and goes back to his own bedroom.

A little later, there is a noise – one small bang. Jay wakes up and turns on his light. He looks around his room. He looks for five things. 1 The bed. 2 The clock. It's 01:23. 3 The snow globes. There are seven on the shelf. One snow globe isn't there. One is on the floor.

Jay gets out of bed. He picks the snow globe up from the floor. It's number eight. It's the new one. He shakes it. Then puts it back on the shelf in its correct place. Then the first snow globe flashes red. Then the second one flashes red. Then the third and so on. Then they all flash yellow.

"Ah! Esme and Captain P are on another trip," thinks Jay.

Suddenly, number eight flashes blue. Jay quickly picks it up. He shakes it. There is no snow. He shakes it again and … there is colour everywhere. He turns around slowly. There are big lines of colour – red, yellow, and blue – in front of him, behind him, above him, and below him. He can't see his bedroom anymore. What's happening? He sees … What does he see? Is it Captain P? Captain P is flying around Jay in a very small circle. Jay doesn't move. Then the colours stop and there is a noise. Is it a door opening? Jay tries to walk, but looks down at the snow.

Think about it …

Jay's dad asks Jay to identify five objects in his bedroom. This technique helps Jay to think about normal things (not his bad dream) and then he feels better. What other ways can you help someone feel better or happier?

2 **quietly** in a way that does not make lots of noise – 4 **bang** a loud noise – 14 **suddenly** quickly and not expected

Chapter 8

"The snow is very bright," thinks Jay. He looks at the snow under his boots. He lifts his left boot up. There is the shape of his boot in the snow! He carefully puts his left foot down in exactly the same place. He takes off his gloves and pushes his hands into the snow. "What? It's hard, but it's soft!" thinks Jay. "It's cold and wet, too." He puts his gloves back on and draws the letter 'J' into the snow. Finally, he looks up. There are his friends. They're smiling at him. He smiles back.

"Welcome Jay! Thank you for coming! I'm pleased you're helping me again today!" says Esme.

"Nice to see you! Nice to see you!" sings Captain P. He's wearing a wool green hat and scarf.

Jay looks down at the snow again. He starts writing the next two letters of his name. He's writing his name in the snow – real snow! He can't believe it.

20 **to lift** to move sth from a low position to a high position

Then there is an angry voice.

"What are you doing here? Can I help you?" shouts a woman. She is standing next to a big car.

"The same questions!" thinks Esme. She calls to the woman: "Hello there! Nice to meet you! My name's Esme. I often visit here. I love this mountain. The trees are beautiful. In fact, there's a very special tree …"

"*My* mountain. *My* trees," says the woman.

"Excuse me? What do you mean?" asks Esme.

"This is my mountain. These are my trees. I own them. You have not got permission to enter here. You can leave through that gate." says the woman. She points to a gate behind the friends.

The gate is large and metal. There is a sign on it. The sign says 'PLEASE DO NOT ENTER' in red capital letters. The gate is in the middle of a new wall which is not yet complete. There are some people working on it.

"Is that … ? Is that a wall?" says Esme.

"Yes, it is. It's *my* wall. This is *my* mountain. My daughter is a skiing champion and she needs to practise every day. We're very busy. We don't have time for other people. She needs to practise now, so please leave. There's the gate."

Esme opens and closes her mouth. She always has the right words, but not this time. She turns and walks to Jay and Captain P. She's worried. How can she check the tree now?

Then there is a scream. "Lilly! Where are you? LILLY!" shouts the woman.

Esme runs back to the woman.

"Lilly isn't in the car. Look! She isn't there! Where is she? Where's my daughter?" says the woman.

"I can find her. Let me help you," offers Esme.

The woman is quiet. She nods. Esme talks to her and the people building the wall. They're making a plan.

---

11 **permission** the legal right to do sth – 13 **metal** strong, hard and shiny – 19 **champion** sb who wins an important competition – 25 **scream** a loud, high cry because sb is scared

Jay is still looking at his name in the snow. Then he sees some footprints. They aren't his footsteps. He follows them and walks down the mountain to the town.

Think about it…

What do you think Esme is trying to explain to the woman?

2 **footprint** mark made by feet in soft ground

Chapter 9

The town is at the bottom of the mountain and next to a big, green lake. There is a wide street with a lot of shops in the middle of the town. Many tourists visit the town because of the mountain, the lake, and the people. They are very friendly. In the summer, people enjoy walking and cycling in the mountain or sailing on the lake. In the winter, people enjoy skiing and snowboarding on the mountain and skating on the lake. It's a great place.

Today, it's a cold but sunny afternoon. Jay follows the footprints through the snow, but then they stop. There aren't any footprints in the town. He walks into the town and looks in the shop windows: local food, wooden toys, clothes, souvenirs, bookshop, and a bike shop. There are mountain bikes in the window. They're different to his BMX. He goes inside.

The shopkeeper and a girl are talking.

21 **tourist** sb visiting a place for their holiday – 30 **mountain bike** a bike designed to use in the mountains – 32 **shopkeeper** sb who owns a shop

"What?! You can't ride a bike! You're a famous skier, but you can't ride a bike?" the shopkeeper asks.

The girl laughs: "Skiing is my favourite sport, but I like lots of other sports. I would love to ride a bike."

"Well, there isn't any snow in the summer, so you can ride a bike then. My kids go. They're your age. They go over jumps or have races. They prefer mountain biking to skiing! Would you like to go with them?"

"Yes, please! I don't have a lot of friends. Thank you!" says the girl.

"No problem! They're at the lake now, but here's a video of them on their bikes. Look!" says the shopkeeper. He plays her a video on his phone. Then he sees Jay. "Hello! Do you like bikes, too? Any videos?"

The girl laughs again. Jay nods. He takes the shopkeeper's phone and searches for his videos online. Then he shows them the video of his BMX jumps in the park.

The shopkeeper and the girl both say "Wow!"

"Well, this young man can teach you, Lilly!" says the shopkeeper. "Can you ski?" he asks Jay.

Jay shakes his head.

"Great! You can teach each other," says the shopkeeper.

Lilly and Jay look at each other and smile. Jay's face goes red and he looks at the floor.

Another phone in the shop rings. The shopkeeper goes to answer it. Lilly smiles at Jay again. His face goes red again.

The shopkeeper walks back to them.

"My friend Esme is on the phone. Lilly, your mum is worried about you. Let's go and meet her. We can talk about bikes later."

Lilly's face goes red now. She's in trouble. It isn't the first time.

"And you must be, Jay. I'm Ted. Come on. My car is outside. We'll get my kids on the way."

---

30 **to be in trouble** to be in a difficult situation

They go to the lake and then the mountain. It's a short car journey, but they all talk and laugh like old friends.

Think about it...

Are there any sports or activities you would like to learn? Do you know any sports or activities that you can teach to a friend?

Chapter 10

"Friends are very important," says Esme. She points to Lilly. Captain P is sitting on her shoulder and singing. Ted's children are teaching Jay a dance. Jay isn't a good dancer. Lilly is making a video of it. They are all laughing.

"Yes," agrees Lilly's mum. "The mountain is a wonderful place for friends – especially new friends." She smiles at Esme and Ted. "Thank you for your help."

"No problem. Friends help each other," says Ted. "Oh, can Lilly go mountain biking with my kids in the summer? You know, when there isn't any snow or skiing. Jay can teach her. He's an amazing BMX rider."

They look at the dancing friends again.

"Well, he's an amazing BMX rider, but he's an awful dancer." Ted laughs. Then he sees some other people. They are carrying things to a lorry. Is that a wall? Is that a large gate with a sign? He isn't sure. The people wave to Lilly's mum and drive away. Lilly's mum asks Ted about his bike shop and Esme walks quietly into the forest. Jay follows her. Lilly follows Jay.

After a few minutes, Esme stops at a tree. Jay watches. Is she talking to the tree? The tree changes into different colours. It makes a low sound and moves slowly. Is it dancing and singing?

27 **lorry** large vehicle used for moving large or heavy objects

"It's happy!" says Lilly. Esme jumps and turns around. The colours leave the tree. Jay sees Lilly and goes red. Esme smiles at them.

"Yes, it is. Let me tell you about this tree …," she begins and the colours slowly return to the tree.

Later that day, there is a party at the lake. There is lots of food and laughing. Esme is happy about the tree. Lilly is happy with her new friends. Lilly's mum is happy, because Lilly is happy. The mountain is still hers, but she wants to share it with all her new friends.

Finally, the new friends say bye. Jay and Lilly will teach each other their sports soon. Esme will return to the mountain soon. Lilly hugs Jay. His face goes red again. Then something hits Jay's face. He looks around and sees Captain P making another snowball with his feet. Jay quickly starts to make a snowball. He's laughing. He's too slow, because another snowball hits his face. He falls back into the snow, but there isn't any snow. There are colours everywhere – red, yellow, and blue.

Jay sits up. He's in his bed. He looks at his clock. It's 01:23. He looks at the snow globes. There are seven on the shelf. He looks at his hand. He's holding the snow globe. It's number eight. He looks at the snow globe again.

Jay's dad opens the bedroom door.

"Dad! We're inside number eight. Look! There's Captain P, Esme, and Lilly. And me," says Jay.

Jay looks at the snow globe again and shakes it. The snow falls over him and his friends. His dad is sitting on the bed now.

"Look, Dad! We're inside number eight," repeats Jay.

Think about it …

What do you think Esme says to Jay and Lilly about the trees? Jay speaks at the end of the chapter. Is this the first time in the story he speaks?

Activities

Focus on the story

Chapter 1
Match the words to make sentences.

1. Jay gives Esme a   A snow globe.
2. Esme gives Jay a   B big, beautiful bird.
3. Captain P is a   C birthday card and some flowers.

Chapter 2
Are the sentences true (T) or false (F)?

	True	False
1. Jay and his dad live on the first floor.	☐	☐
2. Jay's dad likes lemon cake.	☐	☐
3. Jay has got seven snow globes.	☐	☐

Chapter 3
Complete the sentences with the correct character.

Esme (x2)	Jay	Jay's dad

1. _____ has got a new job.
2. _____ needs an assistant.
3. _____ and _____ go to the park.

Chapter 4

Put the events in the correct order.

_1_   A boy asks Esme and Jay some questions.
___   They all eat lunch together.
___   Esme looks at her 'to do' list.
___   Jay does some jumps on his BMX.

Chapter 5

Choose the correct words to complete the sentences.

1. Esme and Captain P are going on a *plane/trip*.
2. The snow globes flash *red, yellow, and blue/red and yellow*.
3. Jay *wants/doesn't want* to go with Esme and Captain P.

Chapter 6

Choose the correct words to complete the sentences.

1. There are eight special trees in the *rainforest/world*.
2. The boy gives a *good/bad* description of the special trees.
3. The boy *leaves/doesn't leave* with Esme and Captain P.

Chapter 7

Tick the three events from the chapter.
(There are two events that did <u>not</u> happen.)

☐ Jay has a bad dream.
☐ Jay puts one snow globe on the floor.
☐ Jay sees Captain P by the door.
☐ Jay watches the snow globes flash different colours.
☐ Jay's dad leaves Jay's bedroom.

Chapter 8

Who says these statements: Captain P, Esme, or the woman?

1. Let me help you.

2. Nice to see you!

3. Thank you for coming!

4. This is my mountain.

Chapter 9

Complete the sentences.

1. The town is popular with tourists because of

2. The people in the shop are talking about

3. They leave the shop and go to

Chapter 10

Answer the questions.

1. Esme says "friends are important". Do you agree?
2. What do you think Esme tells Lilly and Jay about the tree?
3. How do you think Jay travels home?

Your review

What did you think of the story? Complete the review with your opinions.

What I liked

1.

2.

3.

What I didn't like

1.

2.

3.

My favourite character is _____ because:

My favourite chapter is _____ because:

Stars: _____ / 5

Focus on the characters

1. Look back at *Before you start* and the questions you wrote about the characters. Can you answer the questions now?

2. Choose two characters and write a short description about them.

Character 1

Character 2

Focus on grammar

1. Complete the dialogues with *are*, *aren't* or *is*.

1. A: _____ there a garden at Esme's house?
   B: Yes, there _____. In fact, there _____
   two gardens.

2. A: _____ there seven snow globes?
   B: No, there _____. There _____ eight
   snow globes.

3. A: _____ there a special tree near your home?
   B: Maybe. There _____ special trees around the
   world.

2. Put the adverb of frequency in the correct place.

1. Esme and Captain P visit the special trees. (regularly)
2. Jay's bedroom light is on. (always)
3. Esme and Jay ride their bikes. (often)
4. Jay's dad goes on trips with Esme and Captain P. (never)
5. Jay says any words. (rarely)

3. Choose the correct words.

1. Esme and Captain P *go/are going* on trips together.
2. Jay *hasn't got/haven't got* a new BMX bike.
3. Captain P *is wearing/wear* a pilot uniform today.
4. You can ski, but you *can't/cant* ride a bike.
5. Captain P is very *excited/exciting* about the trip.

Build your vocabulary

Focus on words

1. Find ten words from the story in the puzzle.

cough					finally				helmet				
		permission					quietly				smile		
suddenly				tourist				trouble				whisper	

```
H  C  Y  G  V  G  A  N  A  N  N  W  L  E  R
E  T  T  L  E  U  N  B  O  W  H  O  L  X  A
L  O  D  Z  N  U  O  I  P  I  H  I  Q  R  N
M  B  D  C  L  E  S  F  S  T  M  Y  Q  P  I
E  V  X  E  V  S  D  P  K  S  V  J  Q  T  Y
T  D  J  Z  I  A  E  D  C  J  R  O  Z  D  T
J  Z  O  M  B  R  U  C  U  O  Z  U  M  E  S
J  Q  R  A  C  G  W  X  Y  S  P  W  E  B  I
D  E  C  Z  S  U  X  G  E  I  U  R  A  Z  R
P  S  S  O  P  G  J  L  G  H  D  M  N  P  U
J  U  H  C  U  W  B  F  I  N  A  L  L  Y  O
S  X  N  R  I  G  Y  L  T  E  I  U  Q  Z  T
D  X  S  Z  Q  B  H  T  R  O  U  B  L  E  M
```

2. Write the words for the definitions.

1. a c_____ = a group of the same things
2. l_____ = to move something from a low position to a high position
3. p_____ up = to take something in your hand
4. s_____ your head = to move your head from side to side because you want to say "no"
5. s_____ = no noise
6. s_____ = a situation that is continuing
7. s_____ = quickly and not expected
8. a t_____ = a person visiting a place for their holiday
9. w_____ = to speak in a low, quiet voice
10. w_____ = able to understand things or give advice because of years of experience and knowledge

Look at the mind map. Can you add extra words to each group?

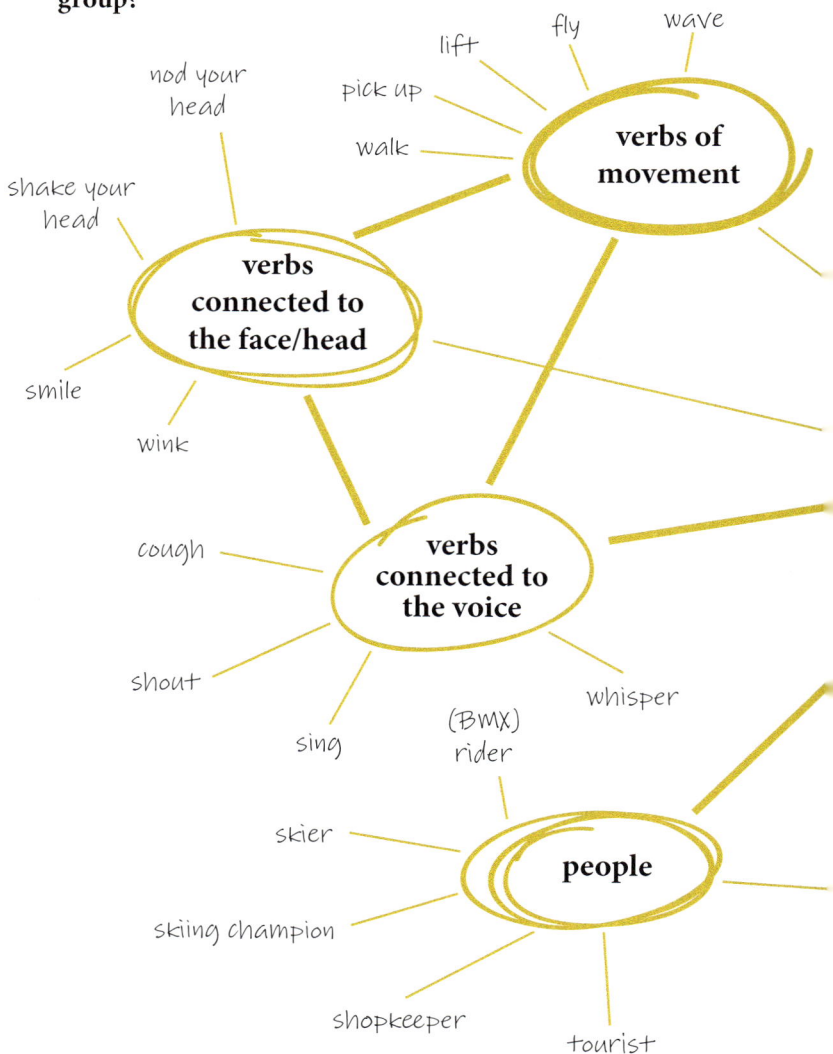

verbs of movement

lift
fly
wave
pick up
walk

verbs connected to the face/head

nod your head
shake your head
smile
wink

verbs connected to the voice

cough
shout
sing
whisper

people

(BMX) rider
skier
skiing champion
shopkeeper
tourist

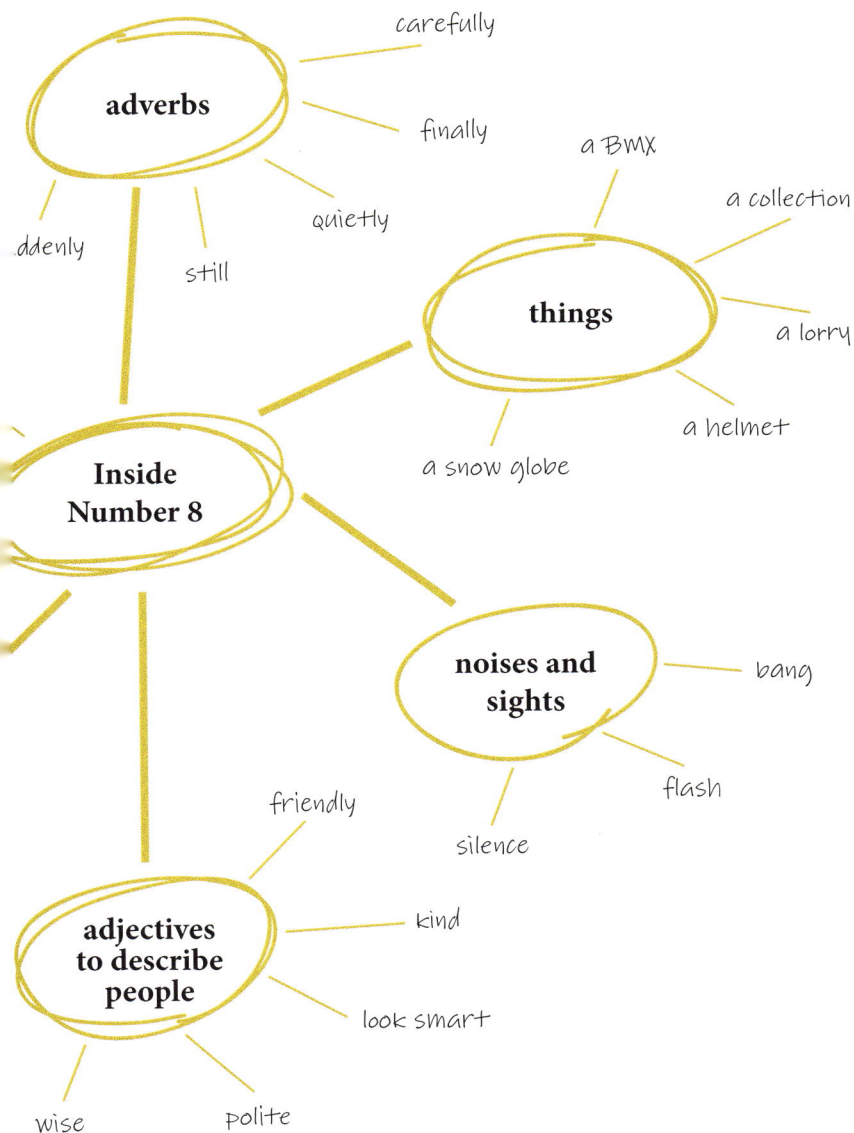

adverbs

- carefully
- finally
- quietly
- ddenly
- still

things

- a BMX
- a collection
- a lorry
- a helmet
- a snow globe

Inside Number 8

noises and sights

- bang
- flash
- silence

adjectives to describe people

- friendly
- kind
- look smart
- wise
- polite

Glossary

	New word?	Notes / connected words
Chapter 1		
smile (v)	☐	
sing (v)	☐	
nod (v)	☐	
wink (v)	☐	
snow globe (n)	☐	
understand (v)	☐	
Chapter 2		
finally (advb)	☐	
bite (n)	☐	
shake (v)	☐	
eh (exclamation)	☐	
pick up (ph.vb)	☐	
collection (n)	☐	
Chapter 3		
smart (adj)	☐	
cough (v)	☐	
formal (adj)	☐	
wise (adj)	☐	
joke (n)	☐	
still (advb)	☐	
wave (v)	☐	
Chapter 4		
jump (n)	☐	
BMX (n)	☐	
rider (n)	☐	
helmet (n)	☐	

	New word?	Notes / connected words
whisper (v)	☐	
tick (n)	☐	

Chapter 5

flash (n)	☐	
silence (n)	☐	
way (n)	☐	

Chapter 6

voice (n)	☐	
departure (n)	☐	

Chapter 7

quietly (advb)	☐	
bang (n)	☐	
suddenly (advb)	☐	

Chapter 8

lift (v)	☐	
permission (n)	☐	
metal (adj)	☐	
champion (n)	☐	

Chapter 9

tourist (n)	☐	
shopkeeper (n)	☐	
trouble (n)	☐	

Chapter 10

lorry (n)	☐	

Find out more

Trees

1. In Chapter 3, the boy in the rainforest explains the importance of trees to the planet. Esme and Captain P know this, because they look after a number of special trees around the world. Can you think of eight ways trees help the planet and/or ways we can protect trees and rainforests?

1.
2.
3.
4.
5.
6.
7.
8.

Continents

2. Esme and Captain P look after eight special trees around the world. How many continents are there in the world? What do you know about each one? Make a poster showing the continents and the countries in each one.

Answer key

Focus on the story

Chapter 1
1. C, 2. A, 3. B

Chapter 2
1. F Jay and his dad live on the **second** floor., 2. T, 3. F Jay has got **eight** snow gloves.

Chapter 3
1. Jay's dad, 2. Esme, 3. Jay, Esme

Chapter 4
2. Jay does some jumps on his BMX., 3. They all eat lunch together., 4. Esme looks at her 'to do' list.

Chapter 5
1. trip, 2. red, yellow, and blue, 3. wants

Chapter 6
1. world, 2. good, 3. doesn't leave

Chapter 7
Jay has a bad dream.
Jay watches the snow globes flash different colours.
Jay's dad leaves Jay's bedroom.

Chapter 8
1. Esme, 2. Captain P, 3. Esme, 4. the woman

Chapter 9
Suggested answers
1. the mountain, the lake, and the people
2. skiing, riding bikes, mountain biking, videos online

3. the lake and the mountain (because Lilly's mum is worried about her)

Chapter 10
1-3 Students' own answers

Focus on grammar

1.
1. Is, is, are, 2. Are, aren't, are, 3. Is, are

2.
1. Esme and Captain P **regularly** visit the special trees.
2. Jay's bedroom light is **always** on.
3. Esme and Jay **often** ride their bikes.
4. Jay's dad **never** goes on trips with Esme and Captain P.
5. Jay **rarely** says any words.

3.
1. go, 2. hasn't got, 3. is wearing, 4. can't, 5. excited

Focus on words

1.

```
H  C  Y  G  V  G  A  N  A  N  N  W  L  E  R
E  T  T  L  E  U  N  B  O  W  H  O  L  X  A
L  O  D  Z  N  U  O  I  P  I  H  I  Q  R  N
M  B  D  C  L  E  S  F  S  T  M  Y  Q  P  I
E  V  X  E  V  S  D  P  K  S  V  J  Q  T  Y
T  D  J  Z  I  A  E  D  C  J  R  O  Z  D  T
J  Z  O  M  B  R  U  C  U  O  Z  U  M  E  S
J  Q  R  A  C  G  W  X  Y  S  P  W  E  B  I
D  E  C  Z  S  U  X  G  E  I  U  R  A  Z  R
P  S  S  O  P  G  J  L  G  H  D  M  N  P  U
J  U  H  C  U  W  B  F  I  N  A  L  L  Y  O
S  X  N  R  I  G  Y  L  T  E  I  U  Q  Z  T
D  X  S  Z  Q  B  H  T  R  O  U  B  L  E  M
```

2.
1. collection, 2. lift, 3. pick, 4. shake, 5. silence, 6. still, 7. suddenly,
8. tourist, 9. whisper, 10. wise